MINIATURE BAPTISMAL FONTS

MINIATURE
BAPTISMAL
FONTS

Julian Wheeler

Fircone Books

First published in 2016 by Fircone Books Ltd
44 Wales Street, Kings Sutton, Banbury OX17 3RR
www.firconebooks.com

ISBN 978 1 907700 08 8

Designed and typeset by Richard Wheeler.
Printed and bound in Wales.

Fircone Books is committed to a sustainable future for our business, our readers and our planet. The book in your
hands is made from paper certified by the Forest Stewardship Council.

British Library Catalogue in Publishing Data.
A CIP catalogue record for this book is available from the British Library.

FRONT COVER: Portable font, possibly by Minton, of c.1842 in white parian-ware (45cm x 22cm).
BACK COVER: C19 alabaster pocket or travelling font and fitted box (6.6cm x 8.3cm).
FRONTISPIECE: Probably C19 limestone miniature font and base of unknown date (c.28cm x 15cm).

Contents

Miniature Delights

THE service of baptism around an ancient church font, with parents and godparents in their best clothes, the babe perhaps in a cherished gown that has done duty for generations, surrounded by relations and friends, is a wondrous experience. As the holy water is sprinkled on the babe's head, will he or she cry out as the devil and all his works are driven out? My mother told me that I did but my sons slept through it all.

But what if the babe cannot be taken to church and is sick at home or in hospital? Why then, the font must be taken to the child. Not the huge medieval stone font but a small portable font. In the 1840s and '50s, with the terrible tide of infant mortality, a number of factories made miniature porcelain fonts, sometimes in special carrying cases and often copied from famous fonts, such as the one in Winchester Cathedral.

Now Julian Wheeler has done a wondrous job in producing a book about these miniature fonts. Not just the ceramic ones like those by the Worcester Porcelain Company that I looked after as Museum curator, but examples ranging from the cheapest in wood up to the finest in gold and silver suitable for Queen Victoria's first born. An enormous amount of research has gone into the making of a fascinating book and the author has even found examples hiding inside church fonts, used by the clergy so that they did not need to fill the whole font with water. What you might think looks like a boring subject turns out to be as exciting as a well-written detective story as the author delves into these miniature delights, and I found myself wanting to collect them.

Henry Sandon, MBE

Preface

AFTER I retired I became interested in medieval baptismal fonts, and decided to make a country-wide study of them with the intention of writing a book. I was admiring one particularly fine Norman font in Warwickshire when I came across a miniature font basin secreted beneath the font cover. I was intrigued. It piqued my curiosity, especially as the local priest and church wardens had no idea of its origin. From then on I was on the look-out for other miniature fonts – or 'fontlets' as they were so delightfully termed by Francis Bond in his book *Fonts and Font Covers*.

This short book is a record of my findings, with as much of the history and background of these fascinating curios as I could find.

I am grateful to all of the relevant parish priests and church wardens for their help, and for permission to take photographs of their treasures. In particular I am indebted to the Dean and Chapter of Winchester Cathedral for allowing access to their replica font, and to the Dean of York Minster for providing details and a photograph of the miniature housed in their treasury.

Thanks are also due to the curator of the Museum of Royal Worcester, and to the ceramics officer at the Potteries Museum & Art Gallery in Stoke on Trent; to Janis Rodwell of the Spode Museum Trust for her generous help with archival material; to Peter Howell for information on the Cambridge Camden Society, and to John Salmon for access to photographs of his collection of miniature fonts.

I will always be grateful to Richard and Su Wheeler of Fircone Books for their expertise, help and advice, especially in acquiring additional photographs and information. Thank you also to Lyn Roberts for reading the manuscript, and to Pippa Wheeler for the use of her atmospheric photograph of the Royal Worcester miniatures.

Indeed, I would like to acknowledge all those who have supported me in this venture.

All dimensions in the book are in centimetres, height x width. At the request of the incumbents, churches containing miniature fonts are not generally identified.

Introduction

B EFORE addressing the subject of miniature fonts it would be
expedient to explore briefly the origins of baptism and its
importance to the Christian faith.

Firstly, it is necessary to understand the fundamental premise
that baptism is God's gift to us in the fight against sin; a sin that
stems from Adam's Original Sin in the Garden of Eden. It is
believed that because of Adam's Fall from Grace all newborns
from then on were tainted, corrupted by Adam's wickedness and
thereby inheritors of his Fallen nature.

In *c.*400 AD, St Augustine affirmed the need for baptism for
the remission of sins, as previously set down in the Nicene Creed.
This sacrament became the rite of passage into the Communion
or membership of the Christian Church. The taint of sin is
washed away in baptism, and thus the font as the vessel of
baptism becomes central to this narrative.

Baptism can be by immersion (entering the water), or by the
essentially similar methods of affusion (pouring) or aspersion
(sprinkling). While much debated, the historical usage of the
various methods appears to overlap chronologically.

Baptism may be by immersion if the font is big enough. As
recently as the late nineteenth century a number of immersion
fonts were installed in our parish churches – for example at
Llanbister in Radnorshire – to accommodate those parishioners
who might otherwise have joined the congregation of the
Baptist Church (Baptists believing both that baptism can only
meaningfully take place if the person to be baptised is old
enough to understand the Scriptures, and that adults should be
baptised by immersion).

It was always thought that immersion was the accepted
method of baptism in the early Christian Church, but this has
been eloquently challenged by the theologian Clement Rogers

Finial in the form of
St Philip baptising
the Eunuch, on the
cover of the silver gilt
portable font made
by goldsmith Richard
Farmer for Charles II in
1660 (*see also p.42*).

in *Baptism and Christian Archaeology*, who argues that affusion or aspersion were even then the accepted methods. Baptism by these means has been favoured in the Western Church since at least the tenth century, and explicit reference is made as early as the first century, in the early Christian *Didache*.

It remains the norm now for the vicar to baptise the baby by affusion or aspersion. This merely entails the vicar pouring a little water over the baby's head, or dipping his fingers in the holy water and sprinkling a few drops on the baby's head, whilst making the sign of the cross. The vessel used to contain the holy water can therefore be the full-sized font, but could equally be a basin of any size. A small portable receptacle gives the vicar more scope to perform the ceremony where he sees fit.

Full-sized font and similarly shaped portable font basin.

History of Miniature Fonts

THERE is evidence that portable fonts were in use at least as early as the sixteenth century, when there were a number of conflicting ecclesiastical directives. In 1549, the *Book of Common Prayer* supported the Tudor rubric of ceremonial immersion at baptism. But by 1558 the Calvinists were encouraging baptism by aspersion or affusion using a basin placed within the main font.

Queen Elizabeth I subsequently became alarmed at the banishing or destruction of ancient fonts as a result of the Reformation. In 1561 she decreed that fonts were to remain in churches; and later, in 1564, that basins were not to be used at all, thereby leading to further confusion.

She reinforced this in 1571, insisting that every church have a font, not a basin ('sacer fons, non pelvis'); and all this in spite of her Protestant beliefs. The Puritans, however, were inclined to ignore her dictums, and continued to promote small metal basins (a comparatively large number of sixteenth-century pewter vessels, for example, survive in Leicestershire and Lincolnshire).

In 1645, Oliver Cromwell issued the 'Commonwealth Directorate of Public Worship'. In effect, this ordered the abolition of all fonts (resulting in the destruction of many more beautiful medieval fonts), with basins to be used instead. With these basins, baptism by aspersion or affusion was to be conducted. At this time, it will be remembered, while Calvinist doctrine favoured the basin, the *Book of Common Prayer* continued to encourage ceremonial immersion. With the restoration of the monarchy in 1660 the main font once more regained its primacy in the service of baptism.

It was in the eighteenth and nineteenth centuries, however, that baptism was elevated to a higher social status, with the ordering of private baptisms by those of position and rank – even though the *Book of Common Prayer* frowned upon the practice.

This new market for portable fonts for use in private baptism seems at least partly to account for the spate of miniature fonts produced in the nineteenth century by the great Staffordshire pottery factories: in particular Wedgwood, Minton, Spode, Copeland and Worcester.

Another important factor in the production of miniature fonts was a demand for small portable or travelling fonts that could be used at the bedside of an infant succumbing to illness during the waves of influenza, cholera, typhoid and typhus that swept across England in the 1830s and 1840s. Such travelling fonts often came with a fitted leather case or box.

A further catalyst for the making of miniature fonts seems to have been a demand for reproduction models for display or even study within the home. The hugely influential Cambridge Camden Society (later the Ecclesiological Society), for example, not only offered such replicas to its members, but actively commissioned their production. In 1840, the price to members of the replica of the Winchester Cathedral font was one guinea. This roughly equates to £100 in today's money, making such an object the preserve of the wealthy.

Pottery was not the only material used in the production of miniature fonts: stone (including marble and alabaster), various metals and even wood can also be found. In terms of metal, pewter, for example, seems to have been favoured in the East Midlands for use in parish churches.

Gold and silver miniature fonts, however, are rare, being generally reserved for the higher echelons of society. Indeed, a gold font was commissioned by the Duke of Portland in 1797 for the baptism of his first grandson (this 'Portland Font' was acquired in 1986 by the British Museum, where it still resides). Miniature fonts made of wood are also scarce.

It is frustrating that so few records appear to survive for how many miniature fonts were produced; nor is it clear in how many churches they are still used. As to the question of how many have survived, this too can never be answered with certainty.

In recent years a number of miniature fonts have been made to commemorate a loved one who has died in Iraq or other wars.

22 ct gold portable font commissioned by the Duke of Portland in 1797, from the workshop of Paul Storr (33cm x 42cm).

These dedication fontlets are commonly of stone or marble, and usually accompanied by an inscription detailing the unhappy circumstances of their commission. Other twentieth-century miniature fonts, sometimes of wood, may be found in hospitals.

The vast majority of fontlets still remaining in our parish churches belong to a golden period of miniature font production in the first half of the nineteenth century – with most emanating from one of the great Staffordshire firms.

Today, it is not uncommon to find a small vessel or basin nestling within the font, hidden below the font cover. This may be a simple bowl from any hardware store or car-boot sale, merely there as a convenience to avoid the need to fill the whole of the font with water at the celebration of baptism.

However, with luck, a specifically designed miniature font or baptismal basin may be concealed, awaiting discovery by the inquisitive visitor to the church.

Types of Miniature Font

T HERE are a number of reasons for having a small font, the most obvious being that it is moveable – in contrast to the full-sized main font, which necessarily remains in a fixed position within the church because of its size and weight. The term 'fontlet' is a catch-all for any miniature font.

While movability is a characteristic common to all miniature fonts or 'fontlets', the specific advantages being sought through this movability – and the precise intention behind their creation – may be further categorised as follows:

PORTABLE FONT

A miniature font that is typically larger and heavier than a travelling font, but smaller and lighter than a full-sized church font. This might be used in a private chapel or baronial hall, where its portability meant it could be moved around or secured in a treasury after use; or for use in a church, to be placed, for example, on the altar or on a table at the chancel steps for the convenience of the priest.

Those portable fonts made for private baptism in the hall or private chapel of a great house were often one-off commissions, and would remain in the house awaiting the arrival of subsequent siblings. Private baptismal ceremonies reflecting social status might be viewed with suspicion, for they could be said to flout the Act of Uniformity of Common Prayer enacted by parliament during the reign of Edward VI (subsequently repealed by Queen Mary, but reinstated by Queen Elizabeth I).

The Act states that the curates of every parish shall warn the people 'that without like great cause and necessity they procure not their children to be baptised at home in their houses', before going on to set out the specific conditions under which such a baptism could take place (*Book of Common Prayer*, 'Ministration

Minton portable font and cover of 1850 in white parian-ware, based on the font in Nottingham St Mary (30cm x 12cm).

of Private Baptism of Children in Houses'). From the beginning of the eighteenth century it appears the aristocracy were wont to bend the rules.

Portable fonts used in churches enabled the priest to involve more fully the whole congregation, rather than just the chosen few standing around the main font, usually situated at the west end of the nave. Like font basins, small portable fonts may also be found and used within the bowl of the main font.

TRAVELLING OR POCKET FONT

A miniature font made specifically to enable a priest to baptise an ailing infant in its own home before he or she succumbed to disease or infection. Before the advent of antibiotics, epidemics of influenza, cholera, typhoid and typhus in the first half of the nineteenth century, for instance, claimed many a child, so a miniature font that could be slipped into a pocket or bag became a necessary part of the priest's armamentarium. It was for just such a scenario that the Worcester porcelain company produced their travelling fonts in response to serious outbreaks

Worcester travelling or pocket font of the 1840s in parian-ware, with fitted case (6cm x 10cm).

of contagious disease in the 1830s and 1840s. Minton likewise produced pocket-sized travelling fonts in the 1850s. Sometimes, owing to their diminutive scale, these are referred to (including by manufacturers) as 'pocket fonts'. Travelling or pocket fonts generally came with their own leather case or box.

FONT BASIN

A vessel in the form of a basin or bowl with a footed base, often kept and used within the bowl of the main font, thereby enabling the priest to avoid the necessity of filling the whole font with water, or to conduct baptism elsewhere in the church.

C19 inscribed baptismal bowl in glazed stoneware (c.5cm x 17cm).

REPLICA OR SOUVENIR FONT

A miniature font produced as a copy of an existing full-sized font. These were generally not intended for baptism – though evidently a number were subsequently appropriated for this use. In the nineteenth century, a number of replica or model fonts were produced essentially to satisfy scholarly admirers of Gothic art (such as the replica of the Winchester Cathedral font, modelled for the Cambridge Camden Society). Other replicas, particularly those of the twentieth century, were designed and sold essentially as souvenirs, often models of famous fonts.

Selection of small C20 replica or souvenir fonts in porcelain, made by Goss China (c.5–10cm high).

Makers of Miniature Fonts

MINTON

THOMAS Minton established his firm in 1789, in Stoke on Trent. Like his rivals, he realised the value of the china clay deposits in Cornwall, setting up the Hendra Company at St Denis in Cornwall, and transporting the 'white gold' to his factories in Staffordshire. Thomas's son Herbert took over the business in 1836 upon the death of his father.

So innovative was Minton that the company was singled out for the prestigious 'Originality and Beauty of Design' award at the Great Exhibition in 1851. It was during this period that parian-ware porcelain was first used by Minton.

Minton enthusiastically embraced the new market for miniature fonts and, in particular, copies of existing full-sized medieval fonts. They may also have been responsible for a further miniature font for which an existing full-sized precedent remains elusive (and may not exist). At least three examples are known to survive, though only the example illustrated retains its lid. The markings on the base are inconclusive; however, more than one authority has suggested Minton as the maker responsible.

This exquisite and weighty octagonal portable font in pearl, white-glazed china has a narrow floral frieze surmounting panels of flower-filled quatrefoils, with eight winged angelic demi-figures at the angles, their features of four different designs. The pedestal has pairs of lights between attached shafts, and quatrefoils above yet more flowers. The font has a wonderfully ornate lid, with cusped and crocketed ribs and a star finial.

This miniature font is of a type probably intended for use in private baptisms – possibly ordered, for example, by the lord of the manor for a christening in his own baronial hall or chapel,

Portable font and cover, possibly by Minton, of c.1842 in white parian-ware (45cm x 22cm); one of at least three examples of this design known to have survived.

and thereafter retained at the manor awaiting the arrival of further offspring.

Although there is no direct evidence, it is quite possible that Minton seized upon the marketing opportunity offered by the news that Queen Victoria and Prince Albert had commissioned the so-called Lily Font for the baptism of their first-born, the Princess Victoria, in 1841 (*see page 43*). It is worth noting that, although differing in their design, the Minton masterpiece and the Lily Font are of similar dimensions.

The Minton archive states that the modeller and sculptor, John Bell (who carried out work for Minton from 1847) was responsible for what is described in the records as 'the Angel Font'. This probably refers to a version of the beautiful marble font in Copenhagen Cathedral in the form of a censing angel holding a scallop shell, by the brilliant Danish sculptor Bertel Thorvaldsen sometime between 1817 and 1838 (and used in 1883 by John Rhind as the model for a similar font in Edinburgh Cathedral). While neither of the two miniature fonts illustrated is marked, it seems likely that they were at least copies of, or inspired by, the Minton version apparently made in *c.*1850.

Two parian-ware miniature fonts based on the C19 angel font in Copenhagen Cathedral, possibly by, or after, modeller and sculptor John Bell for Minton
(*left*: 21.5cm high; *right*: 18.5cm high).

In *c*.1850, the Minton factory turned to the beautiful
fifteenth-century Perpendicular font in St Mary's church in
Nottingham as the template for a number of miniature fonts
(*see also page 6*). These were produced in parian-ware porcelain,
with the window-like blind tracery in the panels mimicking
that found in the original. In addition, each had a lid also with
tracery decoration, topped with one of two finials: a ballflower-
like design, or one resembling an ice-cream cone.

St Mary's church in Nottingham has in its possession a
number of these miniature fonts; however, only one of these still
has its lid. Two of these fontlets were at one time stolen, but they
were rediscovered in an auction house in London, and returned.

The 'ice-cream cone' finial model of the Nottingham font was
produced in *c*.1851, though with a slightly taller lid. This design
became a great favourite, and was almost certainly appropriated
by other pottery factories. Minton, however, generally marked
their work, and for a century from 1842 right up until 1942 the

Minton portable font
and cover of *c*.1850
in white parian-ware
(30cm x 12cm) with
identifying cartouche,
based on the C15
font in the church of
Nottingham St Mary
(*above left*).

company used impressed cyphers to identify the year of manufacture (though, in the case of their replicas of existing medieval fonts, these were identified in a cartouche on the base of the font).

In *c*.1862, the company produced a miniature pocket or travelling version of their 1850 Nottingham St Mary fontlet, this one apparently offered without a lid.

A version of the ornate fourteenth-century font in the church of St Mary Magdalene in Oxford was Minton's next miniature font project. The church itself was blessed with Royal patronage (Edward III ordered the renewal of the north aisle in 1337).

Minton's *c*.1862 'Magdalene' design is based on this font and made of white parian-ware. It is chalice-shaped and has a lid (the latter also topped with the characteristic 'ice-cream cone' finial). Like the Nottingham St Mary's fontlets, the base is embossed with the name of the church within a cartouche.

Interestingly, the *Report of the Cambridge Camden Society* for 1841 lists a model of the Magdalene font as one of four then available through the Society, though the relationship between this and the later Minton version remains unclear.

Tiny Minton pocket or travelling font of *c*.1862, also based on the Nottingham St Mary font (10cm x 6cm).

Minton portable font and cover of *c*.1862 (33cm x 15cm), based on the C14 font in the church of Oxford St Mary Magdalene (*right*).

C19 documents from the Minton archive in Stoke on Trent, listing the miniature fonts available from Minton, together with their prices (*above*: MS 1308; *Below*: MS 3925, c.1870–80).

By the 1870s, Minton was offering an array of miniature fonts, with at least six different designs available both in different sizes (7 inches and 9 inches) and different materials (parian-ware and stoneware). The designs for these do not appear in the surviving shape books in the Minton archive; however, written descriptions survive in at least two sets of records for the 1870s.

In 1876, Minton also made a 'muffin dish' font basin, suitable for use within the main font bowl. It is octagonal with quatrefoils on the panels, four claw feet and a lid with a patée cross finial.

Minton portable baptismal font basin and cover in white parian-ware, 1876 (c.20cm x 20cm).

In 1968 Minton merged with Royal Doulton, and in 1991 the Minton factory closed down. The Minton archive passed to Waterford Wedgwood, who decided to sell it in 2007, only for no sale to take place. In 2010, the Wedgwood Museum Trust foundered, threatening the break-up of the whole collection, including pattern books, manuscripts and thousands of ceramic treasures. A nation-wide appeal, however, was successful, and the future of the archive in this country secured. An adjunct to this was the saving of the Minton archive, which can be viewed at the Stoke on Trent City Archives and online.

SPODE & COPELAND

Josiah Spode founded his company in 1766, but it was his son Josiah II who first gave employment to the young William Copeland in 1784. The two eventually became partners, and the two families were thereby interlinked for seven generations.

In 1833, the Spode Company was bought out by William Taylor Copeland, who formed a partnership with one of his most trusted employees, Thomas Garrett. This association ran until 1847, after which the company was known as W. T. Copeland and Sons. So successful was the company that it exhibited its parian-ware at the Great Exhibition in 1851, having first created this highly vitrified porcelain in 1842.

In 1937, Ronald Copeland (a direct descendant) inherited, through his wife's family, the Trelissick estate overlooking the Fal estuary in Cornwall. In the 1980s his son Spencer moved the Copeland China Collection from Stoke on Trent, where it had been assembled over the preceding decades, to the clean air of Cornwall. In 2013 the whole collection was sold at auction.

In the 1820s, Spode made beautiful little baptismal 'muffin dish' font basins in unglazed mortar stone. These were essentially circular, but with three projections on the rim decorated with the signs of the Trinity: the Cross of the Son, the Dove of the Holy

Spode 'muffin dish' font basin and cover in unglazed mortar stone of c.1820, with signs of the Trinity around its rim (larger version illustrated 23cm x 25cm; smaller version 15cm x 20cm).

Spirit and a Hebrew hieroglyph for God the Father. The convex lid (now sadly often lost) was topped with a plain finial.

This design came in two sizes: the larger version measured 23cm x 25cm, while the still relatively common smaller model measured 15cm x 20cm. Dorset parishes seemed to have had a penchant for the larger variety; indeed it is seldom found in any other county. Both large and small versions were decorated with inverted fleurs-de-lys on their short legs.

Left: Spode 'muffin dish' fontlet and 'tricorn' stand in unglazed mortar stone of *c*.1820. *Right*: Matching Spode baptismal jug or ewer of *c*.1820.

Spode also produced a 'tricorn' stand (14cm x 20cm) for this portable font, with the same signs of the Trinity on the three sides, together with a corresponding jug or ewer, with a handle in the form of Satan as a serpent. Both the stand and the jug are rarely found – though happily a great many Spode 'muffin dish' font basins still exist, and are still in use to this day.

Spode also manufactured a hexagonal unglazed mortar stone portable font, with a lid bearing the same signs of the Trinity and a finial in the form of a bishop's mitre.

In 1833–47, during the Copeland and Garrett period, the same design of hexagonal fontlet appeared in highly glazed Felspar porcelain (Felspar being one of the main components of granite). Sadly, this delightful little font is now comparatively hard to find.

Spode portable font and cover in unglazed mortar stone of *c*.1830 (25cm x 23cm).

Copeland & Garrett portable font and lid in highly glazed Felspar porcelain, made 1833–47 (25cm x 23cm).

Copeland, along with a number of other Staffordshire firms, not only made free-standing designs for its miniature fonts, but also produced scale replicas of a number of medieval fonts.

In *c*.1860, Copeland created a replica of the famous twelfth-century font in Winchester Cathedral. As the main font at Winchester is made of Belgian black marble quarried at Tournai, it was logical for Copeland to use black basalt-ware for its replica. However, white parian-ware was also used.

Copeland's miniature version of the Winchester font measures just 14.5cm x 12.7cm, and is inscribed on the base 'font in the Cathedral of Winchr', and on the underside with 'Copeland'. The decoration mimics the original Tournai font, with doves feeding on grapes and details of the life and times of St Nicholas, deriving from *The Golden Legend* in the mid-thirteenth century. Although it seems clear that this miniature font was essentially offered as a reproduction, it is of note that one such example is used to this day for christenings in a parish church in rural Herefordshire.

One surviving example of the black basalt-ware version can be viewed by appointment in the Triforium Gallery in Winchester Cathedral. It was presented to the Cathedral by the Reverend Richard Le Bas Johnson in 1979.

Copeland parian-ware replica of the Tournai marble font in Winchester Cathedral, dating from *c*.1860 (14.5cm x 12.7cm).

Above: Copeland's miniature versions of the Norman fonts in Winchester Cathedral, in black basalt-ware and white parian-ware (14.5cm x 12.7cm), and the church of St Martin, Fincham, in white parian-ware (*c.*14cm x 14cm).

Right: An extract from Copeland's ceramic statuary catalogue of 1876, showing prices for the Winchester, Fincham and Gothic miniature fonts.

COPELAND'S CERAMIC STATUARY.

MISCELLANEOUS.

	£	s.	d.
Basket, Grecian, Pierced, 8½ inches diameter	1	1	0
Blue Glass Lining for Basket	0	4	0
Wire for Basket	0	2	0
Basket, Wellington, Large	0	12	6
„ „ Small	0	7	0
Baptismal Font, from the original at Winchester, Large	1	5	0
„ „ „ Small	0	18	0
„ Fincham	0	5	6
„ Gothic	0	5	6
Card Tray, Arabesque	0	8	6
„ with Pierced Basket	0	18	0
„ Blue Glass Lining for ditto	0	2	9
Card Tray, Gothic	0	5	6
„ Renaissance	0	8	6
„ „ on Low Foot	0	3	6
Cow, on Plinth, Small	0	3	6
Cat, Small	0	0	6
„ Coloured	0	0	10½
Cornucopia Violet-holder	0	3	0
Cupid Inkstand	0	18	0
Cupid Porter	0	12	0
Ducks (Group of)	0	1	9
Donkey and Panniers	0	4	3
Deer	0	3	6
Dolphin, Bon-bon Stand	0	15	0
Dolphin Salt	0	3	0
„ „ Gilt and Chased	0	4	3
Drum Matchbox	0	1	3
Elephant	0	5	6
Fox	0	4	0
Fox's Head	0	6	0
Fowls (Toy)	0	0	6
„ Coloured	0	1	0
Flemish Extinguisher and Stand	0	1	0
„ „ Gilt and Chased	0	2	3

The Romanesque Tournai marble font in Winchester Cathedral, of c.1150.

The *Report of the Cambridge Camden Society* for 1841, meanwhile, makes reference to four replica fonts available to members of the Society: Winchester, Ancaster, Coton and Oxford St Mary Magdalene. The entry describes the replica of the Winchester font as 'Modelled for the Society', with the Statement of Accounts for December 1840–May 1841 recording a payment of £10.10.0 made on May 5 1840 to Mr Flack ('Modeller to the Society') for 'Modelling Winchester Font', together with a payment of £5.0.0 'To Mr Carter, for drawings of ditto'.

The original full-sized font in Winchester Cathedral is one of only seven twelfth-century black marble fonts to grace our churches here in England. The marble was quarried at Tournai in Belgium, and the font was probably also carved in that country, before being shipped across the English Channel. There are four Tournai fonts in Hampshire, two in Lincolnshire (including the one in Lincoln Cathedral), with a seventh in Ipswich in Suffolk. There is also part of an eighth, again in Ipswich, which was found during excavation of the old town ditch in 1894.

WEDGWOOD

Wedgwood remains one of the best-known names in pottery worldwide. Josiah Wedgwood was born in 1730, and founded his company in the middle of the eighteenth century; and it was Josiah who, in *c.*1775, invented the unglazed black basalt-ware that was used for Wedgwood's miniature fonts. Basalt (from the Latin *basanites*, meaning 'very hard rock') is a dark volcanic rock, which was combined with clay and 10% manganese dioxide, and then kiln-fired twice, producing a fine-grained surface which took a high polish.

One of only six black basalt-ware font bowls made by Wedgwood 1774–1788 (35cm x 56cm).

The factory made only six miniature fonts, between 1774 and 1788. They are all of black basalt-ware, in the form of a large-footed bowl, with the rim of banded reed design, and the bowl itself decorated with drapery festoons suspended from rings.

Three of these six miniature fonts were commissioned by the Whitbread Brewery family. All of them were identical in size (35cm x 56cm) except for one, which was 40cm high and is now in the Lady Lever Art Gallery in Liverpool. This example had been in St Margaret's, Moreton Say in Shropshire from 1783 to 1865. Two are known to be still in parish churches: one in Bedfordshire, and the other in Hertfordshire.

Another was given to Melchbourne church in Bedfordshire in 1786; however, it is thought that this is the same font now to be found in the Buten Museum in Merion, USA, having been auctioned in 1959. The fifth is in the Wedgwood Museum in Barlestone, Staffordshire. The sixth formed part of the Zeitlin Collection, until its auction in Boston, USA in October 2016.

In a parish church in Bedfordshire, the William Whitbread memorial plaque above the Wedgwood bowl highlights the close link between the families of these two companies. This bowl was commissioned in 1783 by Harriet Wedgwood, the daughter of Samuel Whitbread I, the founder of the famous brewery.

Wedgwood black basalt-ware font bowl and stand of 1783, commissioned as a memorial to William Whitbread.

WORCESTER

Worcester porcelain manufacture began in 1751, in premises close to the river Severn. Following the visit of King George III in 1789 a royal warrant was granted, but it was not until much later that the title Royal Worcester was adopted, prior to the formation of the Worcester Royal Porcelain Company in 1862.

Further royal warrants were granted in 1807 and 1808 by the Prince and Princess of Wales respectively. Royal Worcester has now been subsumed within the Portmeirion Group. The Museum of Royal Worcester in the city, the brain-child of Worcester ceramics expert Henry Sandon, remains however a treasure trove of two centuries of the manufacturer's creations.

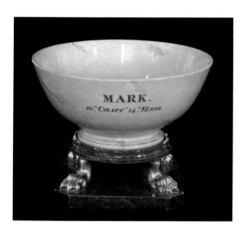

Worcester porcelain font basin of 1815 (*c.*20cm x *c.*20cm).

In 1815 the company made a beautiful porcelain baptismal basin, commissioned for private baptism – an example of which can be found in the Museum of Royal Worcester. The basin looks like a fruit bowl and sits on a base with four gilded claw feet. It is inscribed on one side 'MARK. 10th.CHAPT.r 14th. VERSE.' ('… Suffer the little children to come unto me, and forbid them not: for of such is the Kingdom of God.'); whilst on the other side is 'MATTHEW. 28th.CHAPT.r 19th.VERSE.' ('Go ye therefore, and teach all nations, baptising them in the name of the Father, and of the Son, and of the Holy Ghost').

This miniature font was created for one of the Countess of Huntingdon's private chapels. Selina Hastings, Countess of Huntingdon, was born in 1707 and died in 1791. She became famous as the so-called 'Queen of Methodism', associating closely with John and Charles Wesley, and George Whitfield. She established up to sixty chapels; her religious fervour and Calvinistic Methodism being referred to as 'the Countess of Huntingdon's Connexion'. Her chapel in Bath is currently home to the Museum of Bath Architecture.

In the 1840s, Worcester developed a tiny stemless octagonal pocket or travelling font with gothic roundels on the panels, complete with its own fitted box (*see also page 8*).

The company also offered a similar sized octagonal bowl on a narrow pedestal, and likewise decorated with gothic roundels. Both fontlets are in parian-ware, and examples of both types are on permanent display at the Museum of Royal Worcester.

Worcester was among several companies to produce very similar miniature fonts in the form of a shallow octagonal bowl in white parian-ware porcelain, with blind tracery or low relief decoration on each face, and with four applied claw feet. Although the illustrated example does not have a lid, it seems certain that, like the Minton example (with crocketed ribs and a patée cross finial) together with the unmarked example illustrated on page 29 (with Minton-style 'ice cream cone' finial), this miniature font also once had a lid.

Worcester continued to make pocket or travelling fonts well into the twentieth century, with the boxed example overleaf dating from 1925.

Worcester parian-
ware pocket or
travelling font and
fitted box of 1925
(9cm x 10.5cm).

OTHER MAKERS

Apart from the major pottery factories based in Staffordshire, other less well-known manufacturers were involved in the production of fontlets. As has been shown (for example in *The Parian Phenomenon*), companies such as Thomas Pratt & Sons, 'Church Furnishers of The Strand', retailed these miniature fonts, as did Mr W. Savage of Winchester, from his 'Depot of City Memorials', and J. Shaw & Sons of Longton, each using printed retailer's marks on their wares.

Octagonal parian-ware pocket or travelling font and fitted box by Thomas Pratt & Sons, c.1890 (7.5cm x 10cm).

There were so many smaller pottery factories in Staffordshire in the mid-nineteenth century that it would be foolish to be dogmatic about the provenance of every fontlet. The problem is illustrated by the unmarked miniature font shown opposite. It has four claw feet, each panel decorated with a quatrefoil, and the lid crowned by the characteristic 'ice-cream cone' finial. It is this finial that Minton favoured on some of its miniature fonts, but of course this feature may well have been purloined by other factories. This fontlet is another that appeared in two different sizes: the smaller is 28cm x 23cm, the larger is 28cm x 25.5cm.

This baptismal basin is highlighted in Francis Bond's *Fonts and Font Covers*. Bond writes 'At Street in Somerset, a small octagonal china bowl is in use, each panel containing a quatrefoil; it stands on four feet; the lid is also octagonal, and terminates in a finial'. Frustratingly, he does not say who made it, and no church at Street has such a fontlet today (though this model has been found in another Somerset church).

Octagonal miniature font and cover by an unknown maker, C19 (28cm x 25.5cm).

Other examples of this design can be found in Leicestershire, Northamptonshire, Oxfordshire and Gloucestershire (Forest of Dean). Although the maker remains a mystery, it has been suggested by Henry Sandon that it may be one of the 'second division' factories, possibly Robinson & Leadbeater, established in Stoke on Trent in the middle of the nineteenth century.

Another pottery fontlet from an unidentified factory is a miniature version of a typical Perpendicular font, with paired quatrefoils on the panels, and cusped arches on the stem. The inscription on the base of this miniature font is virtually illegible. Although it was discovered in rural Lincolnshire, its design is similar to that of the redundant late fourteenth-century font at St Lawrence, Evesham in Worcestershire.

Perpendicular Gothic miniature font in pottery by an unknown maker, C19 (18cm x 10cm).

Again unidentified is the maker of a handful of stoneware basins inscribed 'GLOUCESTER CATHEDRAL' and for use 'on the district'. The example illustrated was found in a little church in the Forest of Dean.

Portable font basin in glazed stoneware by an unknown maker (c.5cm x 17cm).

From the late nineteenth century up to the second half of the twentieth there was a demand for replica fontlets, based on various noteworthy parish church fonts – and even on some cathedral fonts, such as those at Winchester and Hereford. Those advertised, for example, to members of the Cambridge Camden Society in the 1840s, were relatively expensive, and were possibly intended more as academic artefacts; as manifestations of the study of Gothic art and architecture, and thus demonstrations of learning. Those produced later by Goss China, on the other hand, were much cheaper and more widely available, and were clearly intended as souvenirs or keepsakes. Neither such replica, however, was primarily intended for use as a baptismal font.

Three small C20 souvenir fonts by Goss China, based on the full-sized fonts at (*left to right*) Canterbury St Martin (7cm x 6.8cm), Avebury St James (9cm x 7.3cm) and Hereford Cathedral (9.8cm x 9cm).

William Henry Goss (onetime chief artist at Copeland) effectively began the souvenir trade in pottery in the late nineteenth century. Working from his Falcon pottery factory in Stoke on Trent, he was ideally placed to provide for the niche market in replica fonts, and the firm produced numerous examples, based on fonts from as far afield as Cornwall in the south-west and Norfolk in East Anglia. These trinkets were for display, on the mantelpiece of one's home for example, being small and relatively inexpensive, sometimes with simple transfer-printed decoration or text (*see also page 9*).

Royal Doulton (established in 1815) also produced miniature fonts in the twentieth century. The firm's 1931 design (modelled by Mary Rutter, and signed 'MR' on the base) is somewhat akin to a Corinthian capital or Roman wellhead, with octagonal top and base, and decorated with foliage, cherubs' heads and scrolls. The design was available in at least two finishes, including brown and sage green glazed stoneware, its bowl lined with blue glaze.

Nor were replica fonts confined to this country. In the 1960s and '70s, the Danish pottery firm Michael Anderson & Sonner produced a replica of the famous Romanesque font in the Aakirke on Bornholm. The replica was available in a brown or white earthenware finish, its bowl again lined with a blue glaze.

Royal Doulton Lambeth 'Cherub' font in glazed stoneware of 1931 (14.5cm x 16.5cm).

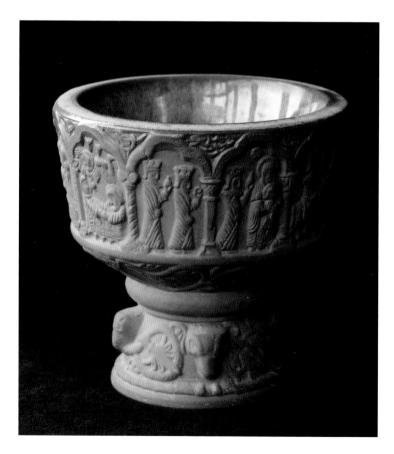

Michael Anderson & Sonner replica of the Aakirke font on Bornholm, in glazed earthenware, C20 (c.15cm x 15cm).

Other Materials

STONE

MANY miniature fonts are made of stone, varying greatly in shape and size, and probably often representing one-offs. The vessels may be circular, hexagonal or octagonal in form, and may or may not have a stem. Embellishments might include a cross on one panel, or the sacred IHS monogram; the more elaborate examples have panels carved with quatrefoils, and perhaps a Tudor Rose or other flora. Some craftsmen were more adventurous than others, carving shields on their fontlets, and giving them the appearance of a recognisable font.

The mason's skill would be further tested if the commission required him to model a more elaborate fourteenth- or fifteenth-century font design; of octagonal section with a stem, for example, and decorated, typically, with cusped arches.

Other miniature stone fonts also seek to copy existing full-sized fonts. There are at least two known miniature versions of the great Norman font at Darenth in north Kent (*see page 34*). The original dates from *c.*1140, and is decorated with an arcade; its eight arches frame a series of images carved in low relief, including baptism by total immersion, a figure confronting a dragon, a lion, a gryphon, Sagittarius, King David, a mythical beast and a figure holding up a fan or flabellum.

One of the Darenth miniature fonts is carved in stone and sits enigmatically in a church in the south-west corner of the Forest of Dean in Gloucestershire. The images on this replica font even follow the same order as those found on the original twelfth-century Romanesque bowl. The second is a pottery replica, 10cm high and quaintly painted; once again the images are in the same sequence as seen on the twelfth-century font. This one may have been intended as a souvenir.

A variety of mainly C19 miniature stone fonts of hexagonal or octagonal form; some with stems, some without; some plain, some with relief decoration; all unmarked. They range in height from *c.*7cm to *c.*30cm.

Above left to right:
The *c.*1140 Norman font in the church of St Margaret of Antioch in Darenth in Kent; miniature copy in stone, with stem (*c.*23cm x 15cm); miniature copy in stoneware, stemless (*c.*10cm x 12cm).

Another accurate copy of an existing font is the replica of the font in Brooke church in Norfolk. East Anglia proudly boasts the majority of that beautiful group of Perpendicular fonts from the fifteenth century known as the 'Seven Sacraments Fonts'. The images around the bowl represent the seven Holy Sacraments of the Roman Catholic Church, with the eighth side variously carved with Christ in Glory, the Baptism of Jesus, the Madonna and Child, the Crucifixion or the Holy Trinity.

It is remarkable that any were left undamaged as Oliver Cromwell wreaked his iconoclasm in the mid-seventeenth century. Sadly, however, many were defaced by his henchman William Dowsing in 1643.

In 1850, the incumbent vicar commissioned an Italian craftsman to create a replica of the fine Seven Sacraments font at Brooke. It stands 23cm high, with the original colour still in good condition. This is the only known example of a replica of a Seven Sacraments font (though other examples may yet come to light). It can be viewed at the church by appointment.

Miniature version of the font in the church of St Peter at Brooke in Norfolk, 1850 (23cm x 15cm).

Remarkably few fonts survive from the period of Cromwell's Commonwealth, but two miniature fonts thought to belong to the mid-seventeenth century can be found in the West Midlands: one in Herefordshire and the other in neighbouring Worcestershire. The former has an urn-shaped bowl, and is supported on a base with an angel holding a book. It is inscribed 'suffer the little children to come unto me, forbid them not'.

A second seventeenth-century miniature font, now in a church in the lee of the Malvern Hills, is freestanding and without the angelic support. It is possible that both hail from the same maker. These miniature fonts are not marked, and were most probably made by local stonemasons in response to individual requests.

Also unmarked is a curious artefact in Herefordshire's famous church of St David at Kilpeck. Here, displayed in the chancel, is a melon-shaped piece of local sandstone carved with the interlace pattern so beloved of the craftsmen of the twelfth-century Herefordshire School of Romanesque Sculpture. It has been described as a font stopper, and this is supported by a photograph in George Marshall's 1949 book *Fonts in Herefordshire*. This shows the stopper, but with the vital addition of a 5cm stumpy projection protruding from the centre of the base, which would have acted as the plug. The Kilpeck font is also Norman, but not of the Herefordshire School. Its drainage hole has since been drastically narrowed in order to accommodate a small metal plug.

It was noted by William Sawyer in *The Gentleman's Magazine* of 1833 that the Kilpeck font stopper had been hollowed out from the top, resulting in a cavity 10cm deep and 8cm in diameter. Sandstone is porous, and Marshall suggests that the cavity may have accommodated a small, fitted vessel, possibly of stone, china or metal, in order to give a usable miniature font. Marshall considers the appropriation of the stopper as a miniature font may have taken place following the Commonwealth, when small basins were used in preference to full-sized fonts in parish churches.

Two portable C17 limestone fonts (*top c.30cm x 28cm; below c.25cm x 22cm*).

C12 sandstone font stopper, hollowed out for use as a miniature font, Kilpeck St David (*16cm x 20cm*).

MARBLE & ALABASTER

In the case of a number of eighteenth- and nineteenth-century miniature fonts, marble or alabaster was the material of choice.

Pride of place in this group must go to the extraordinary miniature font and font cover at Lullingstone Castle in Kent. Next to the Tudor manor house and ornamental lake is the little whitewashed church, inside of which is the pentagonal marble fontlet, square at the back but arrow-headed at the front. It is enclosed in a tall wooden case with hinged doors and a top resembling a pagoda. It dates from the reign of Queen Anne in the early eighteenth century.

Miniature early C18 pentagonal marble font and elaborate wooden stand (font 7.5cm x c.20cm).

Then there are a number of nineteenth-century marble fontlets with the form of a free-standing bowl. These are less numerous than those with a narrow column or base. As they are unmarked (unlike the pottery miniatures from Staffordshire) it is generally impossible to identify where they were produced or who commissioned them. One example was discovered in Cornwall, and is in the form of a small roundish, rough-hewn black basin, otherwise quite plain. It is just 7.5cm high (*opposite, top left*).

A number of probably nineteenth-century marble fontlets with pedestals also survive. Most are between 12cm and 15cm in height. They are generally plain, but are occasionally inscribed with the IHS motif. They are not restricted to one particular colour, and may be ornately mounted. A black example is now housed in the Castle Cary Museum in Somerset.

An octagonal marble example found in Yorkshire closely resembles a number of stone fontlets, even down to the commonly found IHS motif.

In a parish church in the lee of the Long Mynd in south Shropshire is a late Georgian or early Victorian marble fontlet. It measures 30.5cm x 20cm, its octagonal basin narrowing through

its stem, before expanding again to its base (*above, centre of bottom row*). The lid is missing its finial. It has no manufacturer's mark, and again may be a one-off. It is remarkably heavy, and may be another example of a miniature font commissioned for private baptism (possibly in one of Shropshire's great country houses).

An alabaster travelling font found in Herefordshire is just 7cm high (*above, bottom right*). It takes the form of a plain cylindrical bowl, and comes with a leather case to protect it during carriage.

A range of C19 miniature marble or alabaster fonts, mostly circular in section, with stems and unmarked. They range in height from c.7cm to c.30cm.

C19 alabaster pocket
or travelling font
and fitted box
(6.6cm x 8.3cm).

METAL

Small metal basins also became popular in the early nineteenth century, most frequently made of pewter. In Lincolnshire in the early nineteenth century, a veritable rash of pewter basins was produced by an unknown maker. These baptismal basins came in a number of similar styles.

A range of early C19 pewter font bowls (c.7.5–15cm x 20cm).

The most commonly found design takes the form of a shallow circular bowl 7.5cm x 20cm, with an octagonal or circular brim with the inscription 'Parish of … Co. Lincoln', and the date '1819' if octagonal; '1820' if circular. Another simpler variant takes the form of a circular bowl but with no brim, and the inscription on the side; a third type, again a circular shallow bowl but with a narrow stem and base.

Quirkily, a number of these Lincolnshire pewter basins are to be found in churches other than the one to which the inscription applies. In one instance the vessel had understandably migrated from a redundant chapel a mile away; but in another case the basin originated in a church at least fifty miles distant!

In Cumbria in 1838 the vicar even had his name inscribed on the pewter basin. In this case the little basin (5cm x 20cm) sits within a second basin, which itself is attached to a narrow downpipe draining into the main font. The engraving adds, tellingly, that it is to be used 'beyond the altar rails'. Chichester Cathedral treasury also houses a plain eighteenth-century pewter baptismal basin (11cm x 25cm). This came from the church of St James at Ashurst, in the Weald, north of Steyning.

In Herefordshire a number of earlier pewter basins survive, these ones dating from the eighteenth century. They are generally similar in appearance to those found in Lincolnshire, but these were made in London, and in the case of at least two have the name of the parish inscribed on the rim.

A small number of silver baptismal basins also survive. The superb silver basin at Audlem in Cheshire (10cm x 25cm) was presented to the church in 1744, by the widow of the vicar who had been the incumbent for thirty-five years. The inscription on the underside gives details of this bequest and adds 'For the more decent celebration of the Holy Sacrament of Baptism in the Parish Church of Audlem'.

The Chapter House treasury of Oxford's Christ Church Cathedral displays a fine, footed silver christening bowl, presented as a private donation in 1766. It is now used for every baptism as, strangely, there is no other font in the Cathedral (there was once a small octagonal Perpendicular font in the south aisle, but this was banished to the churchyard from where it appears to have vanished).

Silver christening bowl of 1766, Christ Church Cathedral Treasury, Oxford; on permanent loan from the church of St Mary, Reading (20cm x 20cm).

A smaller number of higher status miniature fonts, this time of silver gilt, also survive. The most notable of these include two fonts created for, and used by, royalty. The earlier of the two was commissioned by Charles II in 1660 (though never used during his reign). It takes the form of a circular bowl with domed cover mounted on a banded shaft set on a dish-like foot. It is richly chased with flowers and fruits, and surmounted by a finial in the form of St Philip baptising the Eunuch (*see also page VIII*).

Portable font in silver gilt by the goldsmith Richard Farmer, commissioned by Charles II in 1660 (92.5cm high). *See also page VIII for a detail of the finial, and pages 44–45 for a depiction of its use in a royal baptism.*

Portable font in silver gilt, the so-called 'Lily Font', commissioned by Queen Victoria in 1840 and made by goldsmiths Edward Barnard & Sons (43.cm x 43.2cm). *See also pages 44–45 for a depiction of its use in a royal baptism.*

The later of the two, the 'Lily Font', came to general attention in 2013 and again in 2015, when used for the baptisms of Prince George and Princess Charlotte in the Chapel Royal in St James's Palace and the parish church in Sandringham respectively.

This silver gilt font, adorned with eight waterlilies to denote purity and new life, was commissioned by Queen Victoria and Prince Albert in 1840 for the baptism of their first born, the Princess Victoria. Since then it has been used for every royal baptism. It is now kept in the Tower of London as part of the Crown Jewels Exhibition.

Rarer still are miniature fonts made from gold. The finest of these must be that made for the Duke of Portland in 1797, in the workshop of the celebrated goldsmith, Paul Storr (*see page 5*).

Overleaf: 'The Christening of the Prince of Wales, 25 January 1842' by Sir George Hayter (193cm x 274.5cm). The painting shows the Lily Font being used for the baptism, set within and upon the earlier royal font made for Charles II in 1660.

Silver gilt table salt by H. Williamson & Co. of Sheffield, probably c.1850 (9.1cm x 7.3cm). Apparently bought for use as a font for baptism in the home, it was presented to the assistant curate of St Lukes, Leeds in 1854, then gifted to York Minster in 1976. The design is close to that of the font in St Mary Magdalene, Oxford (*see page 14*).

Any receptacle could of course be used for the water at a baptism. It is no surprise therefore to find that the beautiful silver portable font now in the treasury at York Minster was initially a table salt. The fact that it is in the form of a fourteenth-century octagonal font (almost identical in its design to the font at St Mary's in Oxford, which formed the template for miniatures by Minton) may have persuaded its owner that the alternative use was appropriate, and to donate it to a church in Leeds, from where it was given to the Minster. Being easily portable, it is now available for use by the priest anywhere in the building.

More recently, stainless steel has occasionally been used in the production of baptismal basins – most notably by the Keswick School of Industrial Art in Cumbria. This privately funded workshop produced many fine ecclesiastical artefacts in the years from 1884 until it closed in 1984. A notable piece is the Arts and Crafts baptismal basin engraved with the Keswick motif of a bell, a bird, a fish and a tree, around a cross.

Left: C20 stainless steel baptismal basin by the Keswick School of Industrial Art (10cm x 24cm). *Right*: C20 silver-plated baptismal basin and case (6cm x 13cm).

Wood

Wooden fonts have always been rare. One of the only remaining medieval wooden fonts is in the church of St Andrew at Marks Tey in Essex. Likewise, just a handful of wooden miniatures were made, most in the nineteenth and twentieth centuries.

These include a finely carved pair of Perpendicular style fontlets, one of which is strikingly similar to the parian-ware example made by Minton (*see page 10 and cover*), an octagonal font basin in walnut, and a miniature Romanesque-style font, crudely carved and containing a small blue-glazed pottery vessel.

The Royal Collection also includes a smaller and more rustic miniature font made, unusually, of pith or plant fibre. The vessel (again with an inner bowl) mixes a Perpendicular form with Romanesque decoration, and thus is likely to be an invention rather than an accurate replica of an existing full-sized font.

Below, clockwise from top left: A pair of finely carved C19 miniature fonts (17.4cm and 16.5cm high), one almost identical to the example on page 10; C19 octagonal walnut font bowl (10cm x 30.5cm); C20 chalice-shaped miniature font from an NHS hospital (24cm x 17cm); C19 miniature font made of pith or plant fibre (12cm x 10cm); C19 or C20 Romanesque style miniature font with glazed pottery bowl (c.12cm x 6cm).

Further Reading

Atterbury, Paul (ed.), *The Parian Phenomenon* (Richard Dennis, 1989).

Atterbury, Paul, and Batkin, Maureen, *The Dictionary of Minton* (Antique Collector's Club, 1990).

Bond, Francis, *Fonts and Font Covers* (Henry Frowde, 1908).

Bonhams, *The Contents of Trelissick House including the Copeland China Collection* (Bonhams, 2013).

Cambridge Camden Society, *Report of the Cambridge Camden Society* (Cambridge Camden Society, 1840–41).

Copeland, Robert, *Ceramic Bygones* (Shire, 2000).

—; *Spode and Copeland Marks and Other Intelligence* (Studio Vista, 1997).

Eden, Cecil H., *Black Tournai Fonts in England* (Elliot Stock, 1909).

Godden, Geoffrey A., *Minton Pottery and Porcelain of the First Period 1793–1850* (Herbert Jenkins Ltd., 1968).

Hughes, G. Bernard, *English Porcelain and Bone China 1743–1850* (Lutterworth Press, 1955).

Jones, Joan, *Minton — The First Two Hundred Years of Design and Production* (Swan Hill Press, 1993).

Marshall, George, FSA, *Fonts in Herefordshire Parts I, II & III*, (The Woolhope Naturalists Field Club, 1948–51).

Mee, Arthur, *'The Kings England'* series (Hodder and Stoughton).

Paley, F. A., *Illustrations of Baptismal Fonts* (John Van Voorst, 1844).

Pevsner, Nikolaus, *et al.*, *Buildings of England* series (Penguin and Yale University Press).

Pounds, Norman, *Church Fonts* (Shire, 1995).

Reilly, Robin, *Wedgwood (Volumes 1–2)* (Stockton Press, 1989).

Rogers, Clement, *Baptism and Christian Archaeology* (Clarendon Press, 1903).

Simpson, Francis, *A Series of Ancient Baptismal Fonts Chronologically Arranged* (Septimus Prowett, 1828).

Tyrrell-Green, E., *Baptismal Fonts* (SPCK, 1928).

Wall, C. Charles, *Porches and Fonts* (Wells Garner, Darton & Co., 1912).

Winchester Cathedral Press, *Triforium Gallery Catalogue* (Winchester Cathedral Press).